Masada Revisited II
A Play in Ten Scenes

Arthur Ziffer

April 15, 2013

authorHOUSE®

AuthorHouse™
1663 Liberty Drive
Bloomington, IN 47403
www.authorhouse.com
Phone: 1-800-839-8640

Published by AuthorHouse 07/25/2015

ISBN: 978-1-4772-8964-8 (sc)
ISBN: 978-1-4772-8965-5 (e)

Library of Congress Control Number: 2012922412

Print information available on the last page.

Characters

Decurion

Second

Essene Woman

Essene

Woman 1

Woman 2

Woman 3

Husband of Woman 3

Flavius Silva, Roman commander at Masada

Tiberius Julius Alexander, Roman second-in-command at Masada

Eleazer ben Yair, Jewish commander at Masada

Josephus, author of the book "The Jewish War"

Mark, author of "The Gospel of Mark"

Scene 1

At rise: Sometime during 70 C.E., near the end of the Jewish War (66 C.E. - 70 C.E.) between Rome and the Jews living in what is today the area containing the state of Israel. A Roman Decurion and his second-in-command (Second) are talking after the patrol that the Decurion commands has crucified an Essene in the region between Jerusalem and the Dead Sea.

Second

Decurion, all of our men have been killed. The Jews with their bows and arrows waited until it was light and then picked us off one by one.

Decurion

Are you sure all the men are dead?

Second

Yes I'm sure, Decurion, but the man on the cross is still alive. If we leave now. maybe the Jews will try to cut him down and give us a chance to escape.

Decurion

No they will kill us with their accursed bows and arrows. I should have listened to you yesterday when you said that for us to stay here and wait till the crucified man died was a mistake. We could have made it back to our lines outside Jerusalem last night and been safe.

Second

Yes, we should have just killed the man quickly instead of wasting time to crucify him; and then we could have gotten back to our lines before dawn.

Decurion

Our orders are to crucify every Jew who tries to escape Jerusalem.

Second

But he was a skinny old man who claimed that he was an Essene and not part of the rebellion and was caught by accident in Jerusalem when the fighting started.

Decurion

Orders are orders. That's why I was promoted to Decurion and you not, because our Centurion knew that I would obey orders no matter what.

Second

And now we are going to die.

Decurion

Yes, probably, but I am not going to wait around to be picked off by some cowardly Jews with their bows and arrows. I am going to challenge whoever is out there to fight me one at a time with a sword. (He leaves.)

(After a while, Eleazar ben Yair comes up.)

Eleazar

Your Decurion was a brave man. He fought well with his sword, but he is dead. Now, if you help me get the man you have crucified off the cross, I will not kill you.

Second

Yes, I will help.

Eleazar

Also, I'll need your help in carrying him to a place where he can recuperate.

Second

You mean you are here all alone. You killed nine legionnaires all by yourself.

Eleazar

The bow and arrow can be very effective.

Second

You certainly proved that. But why are you here?

Eleazar

I am on my way to Masada. I am actually going to command there.

Second

Then why are you travelling alone?

Eleazar

On the way there, I wanted to see my mother; I like to be alone when I see her.

Second

But you put yourself at great risk, travelling alone.

Eleazar

Yes, but it might be the last time that I see her.

Second

I understand…. By the way, my mother is Jewish.

Eleazar

What! Do you know that since your mother is Jewish that you are Jewish by Jewish law, even if your father isn't Jewish?

Second

Yes, I know.

Eleazar

The fact that you are Jewish makes me glad that it was your Decurion and not you that came out to fight me.

Second

Thank you. But I can't help but repeat how dangerous it is for you to travel alone. Look, we were ten; without your skill with the bow and arrow, you would be dead.

Eleazar

That's why we Jews use the bow and arrow.

Second

We Romans prefer the sword and to fight in formation like the Greeks. By the way, I am an expert with the sword. It would not have been as easy for you to kill me with the sword as it was to kill the Decurion.

Eleazar

Then that is another reason, besides your being Jewish, that I am glad we did not fight. But enough of this discussion; let's get the man down off the cross. There is an Essene village nearby. If you help me get him there quickly, he might survive; and then you can return to your legion.

Second

Yes, I will, but you have to let me go with you to Masada. I cannot go back to my legion alone; I would probably be executed.

Eleazar

But are you sure you want to come with me? Masada is a strong mountaintop fortress, but you Romans will certainly besiege it.

Second

I know, but at least I will have the chance to die as a Jew. I have been thinking about this for quite a while, and providence has now given me this opportunity. Furthermore, if I go with you to Masada, I can help the men there to improve their sword fighting skills which will be needed against the Romans.

Eleazar

All right, let us go.

Scene 2

At rise: A few days later. The Second and an Essene woman are talking in the Essene village where the Essene from the last scene was brought.

Second

Hello, may I take the liberty of saying that you are a very beautiful woman?

Essene Woman

You're very forward.

Second

I have been waiting for a woman like you my whole life.

Essene Woman

I am an Essene woman and you shouldn't be talking to me like that.

Second

Why not?

Essene Woman

Because it is wrong; it could lead to cohabitation which is sinful.

Second

Who says that?

Essene Woman

The elders of the Essenes.

Second

But how do the Essenes as a group survive if they don't believe in cohabitation?

Essene Woman

By adoption of orphans, and by people joining our group. Also some Essenes marry and cohabit but only to produce children, never for pleasure.

Second

Then tell me, if you don't want men to talk to you, why do you show so much of your beautiful athletic body, much more than any of the other women here do?

Essene Woman

Do I do that? I didn't realize it.

Second

I'm sure deep down in your heart that you do realize it.

Essene Woman

Alright, maybe I do realize it.

Second

Do you know why you expose yourself more than the other women here do?

Essene Woman

I don't know, but I think you think you know and are going to tell me.

Second

Maybe you are not sure you want to live a life of Essene celibacy, and you really want men to approach you.

Essene Woman

Being celibate is not my problem, but I do want to have a baby of my own to love.

Second

So do most women; it is only natural.

Essene woman

But we Essenes are supposed to resist nature.

Second

Not everybody can do that.

Essene Woman

For a Roman legionnaire, you seem very understanding about life and people.

Second

I might be a legionnaire, but I am also a person who tries to understand what life is all about.

Essene Woman

Now that we have talked a while, I think that you are a very interesting man.

Second

Thank you. Do you know that I am going with the man I came here with, Eleazar ben Yair, who will command at Masada, to train the men there to improve their ability to fight with swords?

Essene Woman

Yes I know.

Second

I know this is very sudden, but I don't want to be the only man there without a woman. How do you feel about marrying me and coming with me to Masada, and there together we will produce a baby for you to love?

Essene Woman

What did you say?

Second

I have been noticing you since I've been here. As I said before, you are very beautiful; and, I love you. Please marry me.

Essene Woman

You don't waste any time.

Second

I know what I want.

Essene Woman

Do you have a wife back in Rome?

Second

No.

Essene Woman

Swear.

Second

I swear that I do not have a wife back in Rome or anywhere else for that matter; in fact, I have never been married.

Essene Woman

Have you had many women in your years of campaigning?

Second

No.

Essene Woman

Have you ever forced a woman?

Second

I never did. In fact, I never got promoted to Decurion, which I should have been if promotions were just based on skill and experience, because I was unable ever to bring myself to rape a female captive.

Essene Woman

How is that?

Second

My centurion said to me, "If you can't bring yourself to rape a female captive, then you are not fit to be an officer in a Roman legion."

Essene Woman

I find that hard to believe.

Second

In fact, once in Jerusalem, a woman captive looked at me with imploring eyes, to take her and protect her from all the other legionnaires who were going to rape her. I didn't do it. I feel very guilty about that.

Essene Woman

What would happen to these women captives who were treated so?

Second

Usually they were raped by so many men that they started bleeding out through you know where.

Essene Woman

What would happen then?

Second

The women would usually die.

Essene Woman

So how would it have helped if you had taken that woman who implored you with her eyes?

Second

No other legionnaire would have come near her.

Essene Woman

Why is that?

Second

From my father, who was a legionnaire, I learned the art of sword fighting from earliest childhood on. He was a great teacher and because of that, I was the best swordsman in my legion. No legionnaire would have dared to rape a woman that I was protecting. And by the way, my mother is Jewish, so that makes me officially Jewish.

Essene Woman

Yes it does, but what happened to the woman who implored you with her eyes?

Second

She died. I forced myself to watch from the beginning of her ordeal to the end. She kept looking at me all the time she was being violated. Was not protecting her what you Jews would call a sin of omission?

Essene Woman

I don't know, you should ask a Rabbi.

Second

If I asked several, would they all say the same thing? You Jews are always disagreeing with each other. Do you know why Jerusalem was destroyed?

Essene Woman

Because of Roman might, I suppose.

Second

No, it was the endless fighting of you Jews with each other in the lulls between our, I mean, Roman, attacks. Jerusalem was a very strong fortress and with your water sources within the city walls, the city could have held out for years.

Essene Woman

I believe it. I see how much antagonism there is between the various groups of Jews. As an Essene, I have had much hostility directed at me by Jews of other sects.

Second

Marry me, and I will protect you.

Essene Woman

But we haven't known each other for very long.

Second

Eleazar and I will leave for Masada very soon. There is little time left before I will be gone; and, if you don't marry me now and come with me to Masada, we might never see each other again.

Essene Woman

Yes that's true.

Second

So what about it, will you marry me?

Essene Woman

Alright, I will marry you and go with you to Masada on one condition.

Second

What's the condition?

Essene Woman

That you become Jewish.

Second

But I am Jewish; by Jewish law, since my mother is Jewish, I am Jewish.

Essene Woman

I know that you are officially Jewish, but I mean I want you to start saying our prayers. You know Hebrew, obviously, since you can talk to me; it should be no problem for you to learn our prayers. And, by the way, where did you learn Hebrew?

Second

My Jewish mother made me go to Hebrew school when I was a boy.

Essene Woman

Then you must have learned the prayers there.

Second

Yes I did, and I will start saying them, now that you say you will marry me.

Essene Woman

Good. There is a Rabbi coming here in a couple of days and he can marry us.

Second

Can we start cohabiting now?

Essene Woman

No, certainly not until we are married, and then only for procreation.

Second

Were you conceived by procreation by your parents?

Essene Woman

Yes I was.

Second

Then after we are married, we can cohabit to have this baby you want so badly?

Essene Woman

All right, but remember, only for procreation not for pleasure.

Second

What's wrong with pleasure?

Essene Woman

We Essenes believe that if we are doing something that gives pleasure, then we are doing something sinful. That's why, for example, we don't eat meat.

Second

I get pleasure out of eating meat and I need to eat meat to stay strong. Will you prepare it for me when we are married?

Essene Woman

Yes, but I won't eat it.

Second

That's fine with me.

Essene Woman

I think we understand each other.

Second

Another thing, what is this I hear about the people at Masada that they are mostly members of a group called "The Way"?

Essene Woman

Yes, I have heard that also; they are a strange group of Jews.

Second

Are they sometimes called Jewish Christians?

Essene Woman

Yes.

Second

There seems to be some similarity between you Essenes and the Jewish Christians.

Essene Woman

Yes, there is; both groups believe people should always do what they think is right and not what they feel like doing.

Second

What is the difference between Jewish Christians and the people just called Christians?

Essene Woman

Jewish Christians are usually Jews who have joined The Way, while people called Christians refers mostly to pagans who have joined The Way.

Second

Do we have to join The Way when we get to Masada?

Essene Woman

No, I hear that all Jews are acceptable at Masada.

Second

Good, I am going to Masada to teach the Jews there how to fight Romans and not each other; although you Jews at Jerusalem, when not fighting with each other over what seems to me to be minor religious differences, fought very well against us Romans. If the Jews there could only have fought as one, we, I mean, the Romans, would never have conquered Jerusalem.

Scene 3

At rise: Some days later. The Essene who was rescued in the scene before last is talking to Woman 1 in the Essene village of the last scene.

Essene

Thank you for taking care of me. I might not have survived without you. I don't think many men survive, who have been crucified, even if they are taken off the cross while still alive.

Woman 1

You were gotten off the cross in time and brought to this village quickly.

Essene

But you took care of me. It was several days before I could use my arms.

Woman 1

For a thin man you have very powerful arms and shoulders.

Essene

I have powerful arms and shoulders because I am a carpenter and that's probably why I stayed alive so long on the cross; I was on it for a whole night.

Woman 1

Not to change the subject too abruptly, but are you married? I hear that most Essenes don't marry.

Essene

No I am not married. Though you're correct, most Essenes don't marry. But you should know that. You are living here in an Essene village.

Woman 1

Yes, I know. But I am not an Essene. I am here by accident. I was in Jerusalem when the fighting started and I escaped. This was the first place I reached after leaving Jerusalem and now I am stuck here.

Essene

But you are alive.

Woman 1

But I don't want to be an Essene. I want to get married and have children.

Essene

Then this is not the place for you to be.

Woman 1

Yes, all the Essene men here belong to a group that don't marry.

Essene

Some Essenes get married.

Woman 1

But I haven't been able to convince any of the men here to marry me.

Essene

You're an attractive woman. Why hadn't you gotten married earlier?

Woman 1

In the past, when a man seemed interested in me, for some reason, I would not be interested in him.

Essene

Maybe you never found anybody you really liked.

Woman 1

But I am a woman and maybe I should like a man if he likes me.

Essene

Oh, I don't think that's true. But I am not one to give advice on matters of marriage; I belong to a group of Essenes that doesn't marry.

Woman 1

But isn't the first commandment in Scripture to "Be fruitful and multiply"? Doesn't that mean to get married and have children?

Essene

I am not a Rabbi. I can't answer that question, but I am sure there is an answer. Not everybody wants to get married.

Woman 1

Have you ever been attracted to a woman?

Essene

Well, yes, there were some women that I was attracted to. But I never pursued any of them; I am an Essene.

Woman 1

You said you might not have survived without me after you were taken down off the cross.

Essene

Yes, I did say that.

Woman 1

Then, in a sense, you owe me your life.

Essene

Yes, but then I also owe the man, Eleazar, my life; it was he who got me down off the cross.

Woman 1

I hear it said that you are going with Eleazar to Masada to use your skill as a carpenter to make bows and arrows for the people there.

Essene

Yes, I will go with him to Masada and make bows and arrows.

Woman 1

Then won't that be repayment enough for his saving you from the cross.

Essene

Yes, you could say that.

Woman 1

Then how will you repay me for saving you when you were recuperating after Eleazar got you down off the cross?

Essene

I don't know. What do you suggest?

Woman 1

You can marry me.

Essene

What did you say?

Woman 1

You can marry me. You owe me.

Essene

But I am an Essene.

Woman 1

Have you ever had a woman?

Essene

You shouldn't ask me that.

Woman 1

Please marry me.

Essene

What about trying to get that legionnaire, who helped Eleazar bring me here, and who will go with him to Masada to teach sword fighting, to marry you? It turns out that he has a Jewish mother and is therefore Jewish.

Woman 1

He has found one of the Essene women to marry him. Please marry me. I don't want to die without ever having been married.

Essene

Can I think about it?

Woman 1

No, Eleazar will leave here for Masada tomorrow morning. You have to marry me tonight. There is a Rabbi here now to marry the legionnaire and his Essene woman. He can marry us, as well.

Essene

Tonight!

Woman 1

Yes tonight. And I promise that I will do everything in my power to make you happy.

Essene

Suppose I can't make you happy.

Woman 1

What do you mean by that?

Essene

You know what I mean.

Woman 1

Just marry me and don't worry about making me happy.

Essene

Are you sure?

Woman 1

Yes I'm sure.

Essene

All right! I'll marry you. Let's go find that Rabbi.

Scene 4

At rise: Three years later (in 73 C.E.). Three women of Masada are talking on the last night after the Romans, after building a ramp up to the mountaintop using Jewish slave labor, have finally breached the wall around Masada and will be able to enter the stronghold the next morning.

Woman 2

The high council is meeting to decide what to do when the Romans enter the compound tomorrow morning.

Woman 1

What else is there to do but just surrender?

Woman 2

A lot of the men would rather not be taken alive.

Woman 1

At least they would still live.

Woman 2

No, then they would be crucified. We have held the Romans at bay for three years and they are furious at us for holding out so long, especially with the number of them who got Leprosy from baking three years in the awful heat at the base of this mountain, while we enjoyed the relative coolness of the mountaintop.

Woman 1

Is dying from crucifixion so much more terrible than being killed in other ways, like with a sword?

Woman 2

Yes, it is a very slow and painful way to die.

Woman 1

How so?

Woman 2

Your arms are tied to the crossbeam of the cross and your legs to the upright. When you hang by your arms, you can't breathe. Then you have to lift yourself up by your legs so you can breathe. But then after a while your legs get tired and you have to hang by your arms and can't breathe again. This goes on and on, successively hanging by your arms and not being able to breathe and then having to lift yourself up by your legs to breathe until finally you can't lift yourself up anymore and you die, essentially of slow suffocation.

Woman 3

Now I understand why the Romans break the legs of somebody they have crucified if they want to speed up the dying. But it is a horrible way to die. Why are the Romans so cruel?

Woman 2

They usually only crucify people who have rebelled against them. And they consider our defense here at Masada as rebellion.

Woman 1

So what are the men planning to do and what about the women and children?

Woman 2

The men feel, that rather than let their children be sold as slaves to die slowly working in Roman mines and the women raped repeatedly until they are dead, that each man must put away his wife and children, and then a group of ten of the men will be chosen to kill all the other men, and then one of the ten chosen to kill the other nine, and then finally the last one left kills himself.

Woman 1

But isn't there a Jewish saying "To Life."

Woman 2

Would you rather die slowly in agony or quickly?

Woman 1

I just don't want to die.

Woman 2

You might not have that choice.

Woman 1

I'd kill my husband before I'd let him kill me.

Woman 2

That doesn't sound like you love him.

Woman 1

Yes, that does sound bad; it's just that our marriage has not been a good one.

Woman 3

I think my husband would not kill me if I asked him not to, especially since we have no children.

Woman 2

(Looking at Woman 3.) You're so beautiful; you might be lucky and have a Roman officer take you for himself. But you'd have to survive the initial Roman onslaught.

Woman 3

Yes, you're right. To do that maybe I could stay with the five orphans who hide in a cave? Has the high council decided what to do with them?

Woman 2

I have the feeling the high council will not concern themselves with the orphans.

Woman 3

Then to survive the initial onslaught, I will hide in the cave where the orphans hide and come out after it is over. Also, somebody should look after the orphans.

Woman 1

(Looking at Woman 3.) I have no children either and would also like to survive; maybe I could hide in the cave with you and the orphans.

Woman 2

(Looking at Woman 1.) You are not so beautiful as to catch the eye of a Roman officer. Would you risk being raped to death? There are so many legionnaires who have been here so long without women that they would keep raping you until you died.

Woman 3

(Looking at Woman 1.) Maybe you could avoid that. I would like to have you join me in the cave of the orphans. If we wait until the fighting is over, maybe by then the Romans would be over their initial bloodlust and not rape us.

Woman 1

(Looking at Woman 3.) And I would come out of the cave after you, when the Romans might be so transfixed by your beauty, that they would ignore me.

Woman 2

(Looking at Woman 1.) Would you run the risk of being raped to death?

Woman 1

I don't know.… I have something to tell you both.

Woman 3

Some secret you have; we all have our secrets.

Woman 1

I have never been really sexually satisfied by my husband.

Woman 2

And whose fault is that?

Woman 1

My husband is an Essene and doesn't approve of sexual intercourse.

Woman 3

But not all Essenes are like that.

Woman 1

I know, but my husband is a member of an Essene group that thinks that sexual intercourse is sinful and should be done only for procreation, not for pleasure, and he behaves accordingly.

Woman 2

Then, if I may ask, how come you married him?

Woman 1

I was getting old and men were not looking at me anymore like they used to; and I begged him to marry me, and he agreed.

Woman 2

Has he tried to sexually satisfy you?

Woman 1

He has tried, but it has never worked.

Woman 2

Why is he up here in this stronghold, if he is an Essene?

Woman 1

During the fighting in Jerusalem, he tried to leave the city and was captured by a Roman patrol. They tried to crucify him, tying him to the cross to die. But our commander, Eleazar, on his way here, came upon the crucifixion, and he killed all but one of the legionnaires in the patrol; the one he spared then helped him get my husband-to-be off the cross while he was still alive. Then they brought him to the Essene village, where I was, to recuperate. That is when we met and got married.

Woman 3

So he is here at Masada out of gratitude for his being saved by Eleazar.

Woman 1

Yes, and he brought me here to this isolated mountaintop. I told him we should not come here; that we did not belong here. But he insisted.

Woman 3

(Looking at Woman 1.) Isn't your husband the expert at making bows and arrows?

Woman 1

Yes, he is. (Looking at Woman 3.) And, since, as you might know, your husband is his chief helper. And also sorry to say, they will probably spend all night, ignoring us, making arrows in case there is any fighting tomorrow.

Woman 3

What do you mean, fighting tomorrow? What about the plan for the men to all die after putting away their families?

Woman 2

It seems there is an alternate plan: and that is that the men would put away their wives and children quickly so they won't suffer; but then, instead of killing themselves, the men want to fight and kill as many Romans as they can. They feel they could make it very expensive for the Romans

Woman 3

But what about the fear of being taken alive and crucified?

Woman 2

To avoid the horrible agony of crucifixion, each man will carry a short Sicarii knife, a sica, and will plunge it into his neck to kill himself if he thinks he might be taken alive.

Woman 3

It is beginning to sound like they have decided to dispatch their families but then, rather than kill themselves, fight.

Woman 1

It does sound that way.

Woman 2

I'm sure that they will fight, after having made sure that we, their wives and their children, will have a quick and merciful death and won't suffer unnecessarily; and then, make the Romans pay dearly for those lives. I know my husband.

Woman 3

How do you feel about that?

Woman 2

I trust my husband. I don't want to be raped to death by Roman legionnaires and I certainly don't want my children to die slowly as slaves in Roman mines.

Woman 1

I understand that. (Looking at Woman 3.) Since I told you my secret what is yours?

Woman 3

I don't think my husband thinks that sexual intercourse is sinful, but I have never really been able to surrender myself completely to him. I try and try but it never seems to happen.

Woman 1

Is that why you have no children?

Woman 3

Possibly, but I have known women who have never been able to surrender themselves completely to their husbands who do have children.

Woman 1

(Looking at Woman 3.) You know we are the only two women in the compound who have no children and tonight our husbands will be busy making arrows and will probably leave us to our own devices. Therefore can I presume that you and I are agreed about us hiding out with the orphans in their cave?

Woman 3

Yes.

Woman 1

Then let us go now to the cave of the orphans.

Woman 2

Goodbye my friends and know that I see nothing wrong in what you are planning to do, and God bless you both.

Woman 3

God bless you.

Woman 1

Yes, God bless you.
(They all leave.)

Scene 5

❧

At rise: Later that night. Eleazar ben Yair is addressing the defenders of Masada.

Eleazar

Tonight is our last night of freedom. Tomorrow morning the Romans will surely come through the breach in our wall. Should we surrender? You all know what will happen if we do. Your children will be sold into slavery to work the rest of, what will be, their short lives, dying slowly, bit by bit, of thirst, hunger, overwork, and beatings in Roman mines. Your wives will be raped repeatedly until they are dead, by legionnaires who have been without women for three years. And you men will be crucified…. We can avoid this by first doing something tonight that is very difficult, - yes very difficult. And that is, that each man must dispatch, yes put away, his own wife and children. This way they will die quickly and mercifully. How could any man stand by to see his wife and children taken away from him with the prospect of a horrible death awaiting them when he could have spared them this agony? After doing this, each man will then have a choice: if his grief over having put away his wife and children is greater than his desire for revenge, then he can die with his family. But I know from what I have been hearing from you, that most, if not all, of you will want to make the Romans pay dearly for forcing us to dispatch our loved ones. Now if a man wants to die with his family, let it be so. But for those of you, who want to take some revenge on the Romans, there is a plan to fight. Remember, we are in a good position here, are well armed, and are good fighters. We are especially good with the bow and arrow. We could kill a lot of Romans. With this prospect in mind, the high council has discussed what would be the best way to fight and have come up with the following plan. We start with a tight half-ring around the Roman breach in our wall so that we can kill the Romans as they come through it and before they can get into formation. Further away, on some higher ground, will be stationed our best archers. This will include five women, who happen to be expert archers, and who have indicated that they want to fight with the men. They will be positioned there with their husbands who will be able to make sure that none of their wives will be taken alive. Furthermore, on the higher ground, there will be stockpiles of swords, spears, and, of course, bows and arrows, as well as water. The most difficult part of this plan will be the retreat to the higher ground when a signal is given. This signal to retreat will be given when the Romans break through our half-ring around the breach, and the retreat will be covered by our archers on the higher ground. With the element of surprise, we should be able to allow a large number of our men to make it up to the higher ground to continue fighting. Also, I want every man to carry a sica so that if he thinks he will be captured while still alive and then crucified, he can, if he wishes to, kill himself. Furthermore, if an archer sees a

Jew on the verge of being taken alive, I want that archer to kill him. This way we can deprive the Romans of crucifying any of us. We are the last stronghold of our people; and by what we do here tomorrow, we will teach the Romans what Jewish determination, or, as some say, what "Jewish Iron," is all about. So then I want you all now to go back to your huts and do what has to be done with your families, and then prepare for the Romans coming tomorrow morning. Finally, I want to give all of you the blessing of our one mighty and perfect God and thank you all for having come here to Masada. You didn't have to come here and I thank you one and all for that.

Scene 6

At rise: Second and his Essene wife are talking in their hut.

Second

You know what all the men are doing now.

Essene Woman

Yes I know.

Second

You Jews are tough. To kill one's wife and children cannot be easy.

Essene Woman

You of all people should know why it is necessary. You saw a woman raped to death.

Second

So am I supposed to kill you and our child?

Essene Woman

Yes, if you want us to die quickly and mercifully.

Second

Are you sorry you married me and came here to Masada?

Essene Woman

No.

Second

But you are going to die young.

Essene Woman

But these three years up here at Masada, having a child and living with you, have been glorious. As an Essene I never thought love could be so important.

Second

So you love me?

Essene Woman

Yes.

Second

As much as I love you.

Essene Woman

I love you almost as much as I love our child.

Second

That's to be expected.

Essene Woman

No matter what happens, I am glad I came here with you.

Second

Thank you for saying that.

Essene Woman

Did you mind giving up meat here at Masada, which you said you love?

Second

No, I quickly got used to it, and it seems not to be necessary to eat meat to stay strong.

Essene Woman

To get to something more important than meat, you've made the men here at Masada as expert with the sword as they are with the bow and arrow. Tomorrow when the Romans break through the breach, they are in for a surprise. You did a great thing and I am so glad to have been instrumental in helping you do this by making it easy for you to come to Masada.

Second

Yes, you made it easy for me to live here, but I must say that you Jews were apt pupils.

Essene Woman

Don't say you Jews. You are as much a Jew as anybody here. Your mother is Jewish, so you are officially Jewish. But more than that, you live as a Jew, and therefore you are Jewish if you want to be.

Second

Again, thank you for saying that. But tell me why are we up here. Why did the people here allow themselves to be trapped up here on this mountaintop?

Essene Woman

I've wondered about that myself.

Second

And also who is that old man living apart with his family who keep to themselves? I have a feeling that everyone is here to protect him.

Essene Woman

Since we are not members of The Way, none of the other people here at Masada would ever tell me anything about him, except that he was an important person in The Way, somehow connected with the founding of the movement.

Second

Should we have become members of The Way?

Essene Woman

It wouldn't make any difference now.

Second

Don't you want to know what we are going to die for?

Essene Woman

It would help, but we are still going to die.

Second

You know, I have an idea on how we can survive.

Essene Woman

Oh, why don't you tell me?

Second

You, I, and our child, go down the Snake Path which the Romans don't guard, since it is so difficult a descent, and then make it to the camp of the Jewish slaves that built the ramp up to here, hopefully unnoticed by the Romans.

Essene Woman

And then what?

Second

After Masada is taken, the Romans will probably just disband the slave camp, since the slaves there were not involved in any rebellious activities, and let them fend for themselves; and then we can go to some nearby Essene village.

Essene Woman

Would we go down the Snake Path by ourselves?

Second

Yes.

Essene Woman

Why can't we take others with us?

Second

Firstly, only a small group, namely, we three, with me carrying our child, could do it without making noise and attracting the attention of the Romans; and, secondly, of all the women in the compound, very few have your physical capability to climb down the difficult Snake Path; and, finally, the people here are mostly members of The Way and would not leave Eleazar and that secretive old man they might be here to protect.

Essene Woman

When would we go?

Second

Soon; in fact, we should go shortly after I say goodbye to a few people.

Essene Woman

What happens if we are caught by the Romans?

Second

You know what will happen. Are you willing to risk it?

Essene Woman

Yes.

Second

Then let us prepare to go.

Scene 7

❧

At rise: Still later that night. The Essene and the husband of Woman 3 are talking.

Essene

Well, we are finished with what we had to do. We have distributed all the arrows we made and have built ourselves a little perch here where we can look down on everybody. We should be able to kill a lot of Romans.

Husband

This is a good idea. We can shoot our long bows from here and very few Romans will be able to shoot back. Now, not to change the subject, should we worry about our wives?

Essene

No. They know where we are and would come to us if they wanted to. But I am still worried about the five orphans. Are we doing the right thing by ignoring them?

Husband

Did you speak to Eleazar about them?

Essene

Yes I did, and he said that the high council had decided that only parents of children have the right to kill them, so the orphans will not be dispatched like the other children.

Husband

Maybe our two wives, who have seemed to disappear, will take care of them.

Essene

Yes, I think I overheard some talk about them staying in the cave where the orphans hide out.

Husband

Good. I would hate for the orphans to just be ignored.

Essene

But let us talk about what is going to happen tomorrow. The Romans will enter the compound, probably at dawn. With our long bows we should be able to kill anyone coming through the breach. We should especially try to kill any officers that we see and also anyone wearing a vest, since our arrows fired from a long bow can pierce a vest.

Husband

Not to change the subject again, it is interesting that we two are both together; and both have no children and it seems that neither of us will have to kill his wife.

Essene

Yes that is interesting.

Husband

Do you have any doubts about us killing Romans? It does say in scripture, "Thou Shalt not Kill."

Essene

I have no problem with killing Romans. They could just ignore us on this mountaintop. We are no threat to them. Also scripture says that killing is allowable under certain circumstances; certainly, self-defense is one of the circumstances.

Husband

How do you feel about suicide in order to avoid being taken alive and crucified?

Essene

I have no problem with that. Crucifixion is a horrible way to die and, as you may know, I was almost crucified three years ago.

Husband

You know that I am a Jewish Christian and, to some of us, suicide is considered a sin.

Essene

I'll tell you what, if you wish, and I am able, I can try to kill you and not let the Romans take you alive if you are on the verge of being captured.

Husband

Yes I'd like that, if it is at all possible.

Essene

You know, part of our mission up here is to make sure that no Jew is taken alive. That means if we see that a Jew is going to be captured while still alive that we should kill him. Are you going to be able to do that?

Husband

Yes although, I would find it easier to kill Romans.

Essene

All right, then, you focus on killing Romans and I'll worry about killing Jews who are on the verge of being captured alive.

Husband

Thank you. Do you wonder if, even though that legionnaire whom Eleazar brought with him and who has spent the last three years training our men in the niceties of swordplay, that our men will do well in actual sword combat?

Essene

No I don't wonder. I think the Romans will find that we are as good with the sword as they are. By the way, did you hear that the legionnaire will leave the compound later tonight with his wife and child and go down the Snake Path hoping, and with his knowledge of a Roman camp, to get to the camp of the Jewish slaves, whom the Romans used to build the ramp up to here, there to hide away in that camp and possibly stand a good chance of surviving?

Husband

Yes, I have heard that, but if he is captured he will be tortured to death.

Essene

Yes, but he says that he will make it costly for the Romans as long as he has his sword.

Husband

He is a good man and I hope his plan works. By the way, do you find it interesting that our two wives have become so close?

Essene

It was to be expected since they are the only women up here who have no children.

Husband

I have a confession to make.

Essene

You don't have to confess to me.

Husband

I want to.

Essene

All right go ahead.

Husband

I could never really make my wife happy sexually.

Essene

Maybe it wasn't your fault.

Husband

Yes. She married me too quickly. She was very anxious to get out of her parent's house. Her mother couldn't wait for her to get married.

Essene

Do you know why?

Husband

I think it was because her father couldn't stop staring at her, probably because she is so beautiful; and that made his wife, her mother, very angry. She, my wife-to-be, realized this and she married at her first opportunity, which turned out to be me, to get out of her parent's house.

Essene

But you are so well-matched. She is one of the most beautiful women in the compound and you're a very handsome man, if I can say that without embarrassing you.

Husband

Are you saying she married me because of my appearance, and that she really didn't love me?

Essene

Appearance is very important. Our first king, Saul, was chosen because of his appearance.

Husband

But he turned out to not be a very good king.

Essene

That's true.

Husband

You know it bothered me when you said that I am a very handsome man.

Essene

I'm sorry but you are. I have a confession to make also. Like your wife, my wife has not been happy sexually with me. But it is my fault, not hers.

Husband

Why is that?

Essene

I never had strong feelings for her.

Husband

You know that sometimes I notice you staring at me in a very strange way.

Essene

Yes, I'm sorry about that.

Husband

Is this occasional staring at me one of the reasons why you chose me as your chief helper?

Essene

Yes, but you proved to be very adept at making bows and arrows, and furthermore, you have become the best long bowman in the compound.

Husband

You taught me well.

Essene

I appreciate your saying that.

Husband

Since tonight might be our last night alive, do you want to discuss further your reason for staring at me occasionally?

Essene

Yes and no, but more "no" than "yes."

Husband

I understand. By the way, does it bother you that some Jews feel, since neither of us have any children, that we have violated the law in scripture "Be fruitful and multiply"?

Essene

I've thought about that; and I think I have an answer. Namely, God tries to communicate with man, and man writes down in scripture what he thinks God is telling him. But the words of scripture are only man's approximation of what he thinks God is saying. Isn't it presumptuous of man to feel that his choice of words for what God is saying are the ones that God would choose? Now as far as being fruitful, we have been fruitful. We have been fruitful in that we have produced for Eleazar and all the people up here at Masada, the best possible bows and arrows. Also, as far as multiply is concerned, I have multiplied by training you. And if you survive tomorrow, you will multiply by training your helper, like I have trained you.

Husband

Thank you for explaining that to me.

Essene

It is getting very late. Let us eat and drink and rest a little, so we can do what Eleazar wants us to do when the Romans come through the breach tomorrow.

Husband

Yes we should. I want to thank you for all the time you spent training me.

Essene

As a student, you might have outdone your teacher. You are certainly better with the long bow than I am.

Husband

Thank you for that. And God bless you.

Essene

And God bless you.

Scene 8

At rise: The next evening, after the Romans have captured Masada. The Roman commander, Flavius Silva, his second in command, Tiberius Julius Alexander, and Eleazer ben Yair, commander of Masada, who has been taken alive, are talking.

Silva

(Looking at Eleazar.) All the women and children were dead when we entered the stronghold, except for two women and five children who hid in a cave. Why was that?

Ben Yair

The men decided to dispatch their families so that none would be taken alive and suffer your notorious Roman cruelty, like the women being repeatedly raped and then they, if they were still alive, and their children sold into slavery to work in mines somewhere and never again see the light of day.

Silva

What else would you expect? You kept us here for three years and killed over a thousand legionnaires before we finally won.

Ben Yair

Why did you besiege us? We were no threat to Rome.

Silva

Masada was the last Jewish stronghold, and it was necessary for Roman honor to conquer you.

Ben Yair

So it was necessary for us to make sure our wives and children would not fall into your clutches by dispatching them, and then all the men fight and kill as many Romans legionnaires as they could.

Tiberius

Well you certainly did that.

Silva

It is interesting that Rome has had the most problems at the two furthest ends of the empire, namely Britain in the West and Judaea here in the East, and I have been called upon to fight in both places.

Tiberius

Because you are Rome's greatest general.

Silva

Speaking of generals, and much as I regret the heavy toll you people took on us today, that was a magnificent defense you Jews put on.

Tiberius

Yes, you had a tight but expanding half-ring of swordsman around our breach in your wall and we could not get into formation and use our usual tactics, and our legionnaires were slaughtered as they came through the breach. Then when your half-ring had expanded enough under pressure that we finally could break through, your men quickly retreated in good order to higher ground where there were prepared stockpiles of bows and arrows as well as archers that covered the retreat; and your men's skill with the bow and arrow continued the slaughter of us Romans. I have never seen such deadly accuracy.

Ben Yair

Well, for one, we had three years to practice while you built your ramp to get up here; and, furthermore, during the time of the Maccabees, we Jews were known as the "People of the Bow."

Silva

I noticed that besides the men, you had some women who shot at us with the bow and arrow.

Ben Yair

Yes, there were five women, expert as men with the bow and arrow, to be sure a little lighter bow than what the men use, except for one who was so strong she could shoot with the men's heavier bow, who indicated that they wanted to fight with the men. Although these women started out on the higher ground with the archers and were not part of the original half-ring around the breach.

Silva

Did these women have children?

Ben Yair

Yes!

Silva

What happened to them?

Ben Yair

They were dispatched like all the other children.

Silva

I noticed some men who were very young were also fighting.

Ben Yair

Yes, when a Jewish boy becomes thirteen, there is a ceremony where he officially becomes a man. Some were allowed to fight if they were suitable.

Silva

You Jews seem to like the bow and arrow more than the sword.

Ben Yair

We Jews believe in using the power of our minds rather than the strength of our arms in fighting. Like everybody we started out using a sword to fight. Then we moved up to the spear so a man could kill another man, or a wild animal for that matter, at a distance. Then we developed the sling and that increased the distance a man could kill at. You probably have heard of the story of King David, a normal sized man, who killed the Philistine giant Goliath with one stone from a sling. Finally, we perfected the ultimate modern weapon, the bow and arrow, which helped us to kill so many of your legionnaires. But (Looking at Tiberius.) weren't you born Jewish, and shouldn't you know all this?

Tiberius

Yes, I was born Jewish. In fact the famous Philo of Alexandria was my uncle and my father, his brother, was head of the Jewish community in Alexandria. But I went to Rome when I was very young and became a Roman citizen and then spent my life in the Roman army.

Ben Yair

Weren't you procurator of Judaea for two years over two decades ago?

Tiberius

Yes I was.

Ben Yair

And didn't you have two of the sons of a man named Judas the Galilean, a great religious leader who was the founder of what is called the "Fourth Philosophy," and who also planted the seeds of our eventual revolt against you Romans, crucified?

Tiberius

Yes, I did; they were troublemakers.

Ben Yair

Rome was bleeding us dry with taxation; we had to do something.

Tiberius

It is Rome's prerogative to tax subject peoples.

Ben Yair

And also when you were Prefect of Egypt, you had two thousand Alexandrian Jews killed by the legions. What was your excuse then?

Tiberius

The Alexandrian Jews were being very intransigent; it was necessary to kill some to restore order.

Silva

Enough of this! (Looking at ben Yair.) Tell me about this new form of Judaism, the "Fourth Philosophy", and where does the word "fourth" come from?

Ben Yair

The word "fourth" comes from the fact that originally there were three types of Jews: Sadducees, Pharisees, and Essenes. The "Fourth Philosophy" is a fourth variety sometimes called the "Fourth Way" or just "The Way". As I said before, it was founded by a man named Judas the Galilean, who besides being a religious leader was a political revolutionary and believed in expelling Rome from Judaea.

Silva

What about the other forms of Judaism?

Ben Yair

The Sadducees, who only accept the written law, that is to say what is written in our scriptures, and who reject the oral law, which are expansions and interpretations of the written law, were usually rich Jews in league with you Romans, who controlled the Temple, unfortunately destroyed by your army three years ago.

Tiberius

The Temple was destroyed by you Jews fighting amongst yourselves. Jerusalem was a strong fortress; you could have held out for many more years, what with your underground water supply and invulnerable walls. But when we Romans weren't attacking, you would fight amongst yourselves, destroying your food supplies and killing each other.

Ben Yair

Unfortunately, we Jews are sometimes not only our own best friends but sometimes our own worst enemies.

Silva

Yes, and don't forget that the Romans during the time of Pompey were invited to come here to Judaea because you Jews could not resolve your own differences.

Ben Yair

But we didn't know that you would never leave.

Tiberius

What did you expect?

Ben Yair

At least a gentle rule instead of the excesses of some of your procurators.

Silva

Enough of this arguing! (Looking at ben Yair.) Continue telling me about the other forms of Judaism.

Ben Yair

The Pharisees are another group, very diverse and numerous. They mostly accept both the written and the oral law. The third group, the Essenes, are very otherworldly, mostly concerned with purity and avoidance of pleasure. They are mostly celibate, although some get married; but, once a wife gets pregnant, they abstain from intercourse with her to prove that the object of the marriage was not pleasure but the begetting of children. Also, they are vegetarians for the most part. In fact, the man named James, who became one of the leaders of The Way, was a vegetarian and might have started out as an Essene.

Silva

Not to be too mundane, what is wrong with eating meat?

Ben Yair

Our scriptures say that until the time of Noah, men were not supposed to eat meat. Something about the blood of an animal being sacred. But after the flood that occurred in Noah's time, man was allowed to eat meat, since it was felt that most men could not be vegetarians.

Silva

Soldiers need to eat meat; it makes them strong and better fighters. But to get back to The Way, didn't it split into two groups?

Ben Yair

Yes. After the time of Judas the Galilean, The Way split into two factions. One group was led by the aforementioned man named James, who felt that all the rules and regulations of Judaism had to be obeyed, and that you had to be first an observant Jew in order to be a follower of The Way. Also, many of these were violently opposed to Roman rule, especially the burdensome taxation by Rome. In fact, I, and most of the people here at Masada, are or were followers of The Way.

Tiberius

I've heard it said that James lived to be over ninety before he died.

Ben Yair

Not everybody believes that.

Silva

To get back to The Way, I thought you people here at Masada were Sicarii.

Ben Yair

Confusing as it may be, some people call us Sicarii, some call us followers of The Way, and some even call us Zealots who sometimes were at odds with the Sicarii.

Silva

You said The Way split into two groups, what about the other group?

Ben Yair

The other group of The Way was led by a man named Paul, who felt that The Way should be for all people, even if they were not Jewish. He felt that most of the rules and regulations of traditional Judaism were not necessary to be a good person. He wanted a religion for the pagans that would make them all behave as Jews in what he felt were the important parts of Judaism, namely the morality of the Jews. Also for this group there was an emphasis on the word "Love" and also on the concept of Salvation which I have never understood. People of this group are now called Jewish Christians. Finally, this group, contrary to the inclinations of the other group led by James, leaned in a direction of accommodation with Rome.

Silva

I am confused by all these terms, Christian, Jewish Christian, the Fourth Philosophy, the Fourth Way, The Way, Zealots, Sicarii, and confused also by the differences between them.

Ben Yair

It is confusing, but the terms will eventually sort themselves out.

Silva

I should tell you both, that surprising as it sounds, my wife in Rome has taken to this form of Judaism. Before she became a Jewish Christian, or Christian, as these people are generally called in Rome, and not to burden you both with my personal problems, she was very promiscuous, saying to me, which as you can guess made me very angry, she would not be beautiful forever and didn't want to waste any of her years of beauty. Then when she became a Christian, surprisingly, she stopped being promiscuous, and now she talks forever about spiritual love.

Tiberius

Speaking of promiscuity, it is also common to some Jews.

Silva

Yes, my wife tells me that in the Jewish scriptures there is the mention of King David who was very free with his sexual favors. She tells me about the story of David and Bathsheba. It seems David saw Bathsheba bathing, naked, on her roof, and was so entranced with her that he had her brought to the palace. Not unexpectedly, Bathsheba soon became pregnant, so David had her army husband, Uriah, who was away fighting on some faraway front, brought home so they could blame the pregnancy on him. But her husband would not sleep with her and stayed in the barracks because he felt that since his men were still on the front, he should not sleep with his wife. So, David, as a last resort, had her army husband sent to the most dangerous part of the front and thereby killed in battle, and then David could marry Bathsheba. Everybody blames David for this. My wife says that it was more Bathsheba's doing: she was very beautiful and knew that by bathing on her roof, naked, she would catch the eye of David and be brought to the palace. They were a perfect match: she was not happy with her un-ambitious low-level army officer husband and David was not happy with any of his sons from his other wives becoming king. Solomon was the second child he had with Bathsheba and became a great king after David died.

Tiberius

That is a very interesting interpretation of David and Bathsheba. I have never heard that before. But to get back to your wife, she, like Bathsheba was, is very beautiful. I have seen her in Rome. Did you ever think of divorcing her when she was being unfaithful?

Silva

I thought of it, but I love her too much. But now I will have my revenge. Of the two women and five children here at Masada who hid in a cave until the fighting was over, one of the women is very beautiful. I am going to bring her back with me to Rome and let my wife see what it's like to suffer the agony of jealousy.

Ben Yair

What will happen to the other woman and the five children?

Silva

I will send them to Jerusalem with some gold for the woman

to take care of the children. But we have talked enough. I want to return to my tent and my beautiful Jewess. Ben Yair, I will say goodbye to you. (He leaves.)

Tiberius

You know, you weren't the only Jew to survive here at Masada. You and your men were very effective in killing your own wounded so that none would be taken alive. But there were two besides you who survived.

Ben Yair

Yes I know about those two. What will happen to them?

Tiberius

Silva tells me that Rome wants all male survivors of Masada crucified.

Ben Yair

Would you allow me to kill those two men quickly with a sica? I promise not to use it on myself.

Tiberius

No, Silva would be angry with me.

Ben Yair

I thought you'd say that. Some of us Jews have a saying about people becoming Jews and leaving Judaism, "We gain the best and lose the worst."

Tiberius

I was born Jewish, but I am now a Roman.

Ben Yair

I can see that.

Tiberius

You think I am a terrible person because I fight for Rome, and as procurator was responsible for the crucifixion of two of the sons of Judas the Galilean, and also as Prefect of Egypt responsible for the massacre of some of the Alexandrian Jews.

Ben Yair

Yes I do.

Tiberius

What about the Maccabean king Alexander Jannaeus? He had 800 Pharisees impaled. And furthermore, while they were dying, he had their wives and children killed in front of them. Wasn't that worse than what I did? Also, he aligned himself with the Sadducees who eventually became Roman wards so that they could keep their wealth and maintain their power over the less wealthy Jews.

Ben Yair

As I said before, the Jews can be their own best friends, but sometimes their own worst enemies; and also, they are always changing sides. The king you mentioned, Alexander Jannaeus, was almost destroyed during one of the endless internecine struggles of our people, except for the fact that one group of Pharisees at a critical point came over to his side. But on his deathbed, he told his wife, the Queen, Alexandra Salome, to align herself with the Pharisees, rather than the Sadducees.

Tiberius

Why do you think he did this?

Ben Yair

Either out of guilt over the slaughter of the 800 Pharisees or a realization that the Sadducees only cared about themselves and their other privileged ilk.

Tiberius

You know, my becoming a Roman can't be all that wrong. Many Jews become Roman citizens. Also, I must have some good qualities to have become second in command to Vespasian, who is now emperor of Rome.

Ben Yair

And then you became second in command to his son, Titus, and now second in command to Silva. Aren't you being successively demoted?

Tiberius

I don't care; I have recently contracted Leprosy which as you know is eventually fatal. But before we finish this conversation, there is one question I must ask. Why did you Jews stay up here on this mountaintop? You could have left and melted into the ordinary population and maybe all survived.

Ben Yair

That's a good question.

Tiberius

Did all those people stay here because of you? Are you related to Judas the Galilean? Are you his grandson and therefore, since I think none of his sons are alive, are you now the titular leader of The Way? And were all those people here at Masada your honor guard, and that's why they stayed?

Ben Yair

Is it important for you to know?

Tiberius

Yes, did all these people here at Masada die because they were protecting you as their leader?

Ben Yair

Do you think that I would let almost a thousand Jews die just to protect me? The people here at Masada and I, as their military leader, were protecting someone else: an elderly man who was a very important person in The Way. I, and all these people here, were <u>his</u> honor guard. You notice that there was a separate group of bodies found in one of the palaces; that was his body and that of his family. But don't ask me any questions about him; I will refuse to answer.

Tiberius

Was he possibly Judas the Galilean, who through some convoluted plot managed to survive being crucified as supposedly he was, way back when?

Ben Yair

I am not going to answer any questions about who he was.

Tiberius

All right, but I do have another question for you that I hope you will answer: which of the two groups that The Way has split into, do you personally favor?

Ben Yair

After the deaths of the leaders of the two groups, James and Paul, I lost interest in the controversies between them and decided to let the followers of each group sort out their differences and determine which group, if any, will dominate in the future.

Tiberius

I have the feeling that the followers of Paul will end up being the more dominant.

Ben Yair

It does seem that way.

Ben Yair

So what happens now?

Tiberius

After the legions rest up and refit themselves, we will all go to Jerusalem. I must leave you now and attend to the legions, since, as second in command, I am in charge of logistics.

Scene 9

At Rise: A little while after the final battle at Masada, Second and his Essene wife are living in an Essene village near Jerusalem.

Essene Woman

I feel guilty that we went down the Snake Path ourselves and did not save anybody else from Masada.

Second

We had no choice.

Essene Woman

I know but I still feel guilty.

Second

You Jews feel guilty about everything.

Essene Woman

I told you not to talk like that; you are as Jewish as any Jew. Because you said that I am not going to cohabit with you tonight.

Second

But we are trying to get you pregnant again.

Essene Woman

We can skip a night. Besides the people here stare at me as if I am doing something wrong by cohabiting with you so frequently; it seems in a small village like this, everybody knows everybody else's business.

Second

No, the women stare at you because they are jealous of your beauty, and the men stare at you because they all want you, even if they are Essenes.

Essene Woman

You're probably right and you know what, we are going to have to leave this village and go to a bigger one, or a city even, where we can avoid this small village gossip.

Second

I am ready to go whenever you are. But that brings up something I have been meaning to talk to you about.

Essene Woman

And what is that?

Second

I can't get over how the people at Masada behaved compared to the Jews of Rome where I grew up.

Essene Woman

What do you mean?

Second

You know that even though my father was not Jewish, all our family friends were Jewish, which was my mother's doing, although my father didn't seem to complain.

Essene Woman

Was your father accepted by your mother's friends?

Second

At first not so much but after a while any objection to him seemed to disappear.

Essene Woman

Do you know why?

Second

Well for one, he was a very good man.

Essene Woman

And is there a second reason?

Second

Yes, he not only taught me the art of sword fighting, but any

Jewish boy in the community who wanted to learn. Most of the parents of these boys were grateful for this.

Essene Woman

You were talking about the difference between the Jews at Masada and the ones in Rome.

Second

Yes. Most of the Jewish men I knew in Rome did not seem to be like the men at Masada, who were fighters. The Jewish men in Rome were not fighters but merchants and tradesmen.

Essene Woman

Like some of the men in the big villages and cities here in Judaea.

Second

Yes, but more importantly, most of the wives of these men did not seem like they would allow their husbands to put them and their children away.

Essene Woman

You mean even if they knew the alternative was a horrible death.

Second

They probably would not have allowed themselves to think of that.

Essene Woman

You know, even at Masada, a lot of the women had to be convinced by other women what was in store for them if their husbands did not put them away.

Second

So are the Jews of Rome different than the ones at Masada?

Essene Woman

The differences may be superficial. You notice how good the Jews are as merchants and tradesmen. There is a saying in Scriptures: "Whatever one puts one's hand to, one should do it with all one's might."

Second

Maybe that's why the Jewish community accepted my father, because he was so good as a sword fighter.

Essene Woman

The scriptural command to do what one does with all one's might, which made Jews so good in being merchants and tradesmen, would have transformed them into their doing what had to be done at Masada. Remember some of the people at Masada were merchants and tradesmen before they went to Masada.

Second

I don't see the connection.

Essene Woman

It is hard to explain.

Second

And what about the wives of these Jewish merchants and tradesmen? It seemed to me that to many of the Jewish wives of Rome, the idea of being put away by their husbands was unthinkable. I cannot imagine many of them accepting this. In fact, I think they would have said, when the idea of being killed by their husbands came up, that they would kill their husbands rather than the other way around.

Essene Woman

The wives accepted it at Masada; and, the Roman Jewish wives would have accepted it also when they finally realized it was the best possible option.

Second

I am glad that we escaped from Masada and I did not have to put you and our child away.

Essene Woman

So am I.

Second

I'm glad that you had the physical ability to climb down the Snake Path and the courage to risk being caught alive by the Romans, much as I would have tried to prevent that.

Essene Woman

There is an old saying: that It takes three things to live

the good life: courage, God's grace, and knowledge; but, unfortunately, you need them in that order.

Second

That's interesting and I certainly agree with that.

Essene Woman

Maybe we <u>can</u> cohabit tonight.

Second

Okay. But I am a little tired now.

Essene Woman

You're playing with me now, but I guess I deserve it.

Second

No you don't deserve it. But to get serious, I have been thinking about this for a while and have been waiting for an opportunity to tell you how grateful I am for you to have made it easy for me to go to Masada, and there become part of the fighting heart of Israel. I love you for that, as well, of course, for other reasons.

Essene Woman

I think maybe it is time for us to go to bed.

Second

Yes maybe it is.

Scene 10

⚜

At Rise: Some years after what happened at Masada. Josephus, the man who wrote the book "The Jewish War", that contains the only historical account of what happened at Masada, is talking to the writer of the Gospel of Mark, which many scholars think was the first of the four Gospels (not Matthew) to be written.

Mark

So why do most Jews in Judaea and Galilee, think of you as a traitor?

Josephus

Because of what happened at Jotpata.

Mark

What did happen?

Josephus

Well, I was commander of the Zealot forces in Galilee and also commander of the garrison at Jotpata, which was our last stronghold in the Galilee.

Mark

What, you were commander of the Zealots in Galilee, but yet in your book you talk disapprovingly about the Zealots.

Josephus

In retrospect, I realized that besides certain members of The Way, the Zealots were responsible for the terrible events that occurred which led to the destruction of Jerusalem and the Temple.

Mark

War makes for strange alliances.

Josephus

That's a good way of looking at what happened.

Mark

But go on; tell me what actually happened at Jotpata.

Josephus

The Romans finally broke through our defenses and I, and about forty of my men, hid in a cave, hoping the Romans would not find us. Well they did and they wanted us to come out of the cave and surrender.

Mark

Then what happened.

Josephus

The men decided to not be taken alive for fear of being crucified.

Mark

I understand; crucifixion is a terrible way to die compared to a quick death from a sword or a sica. But go on.

Josephus

I convinced the men to divide up into pairs, draw lots and one kill the other, then form new pairs and continue doing the same. This happened until finally getting down, by luck, or providence, mind you, to me and one other man. Then rather than continue with drawing lots to decide which of us two would kill the other and then the last man would kill himself, I made a pact with the other man to surrender to the Romans in the hopes that I could ingratiate myself with Vespasian, which is what happened.

Mark

What happened to the other man?

Josephus

I lost contact with him and I don't know what happened to him.

Mark

Well it seems that you were just lucky and not a traitor.

I mean you did risk crucifixion, which showed a lot of courage.

Josephus

Thank you for saying that.

Mark

But tell me, as commander of rebel forces in Galilee and commander at Jotpata, did you ever do anything to betray the Jewish cause?

Josephus

No, I swear. All I did was save my life when all was lost.

Mark

Then I don't think you were a traitor, unless you did things in the cave that you shouldn't have, like take advantage of your rank.

Josephus

I might have at various times used my rank in some untoward way, but my survival was accomplished mostly by using my powers of persuasion.

Mark

Well, you did convince Vespasian to let you become his liaison with the Jews.

Josephus

And, in doing so, saved the lives of many Jews.

Mark

It doesn't matter that I don't think you were a traitor, but rather how will you be judged in the future by your fellow Jews.

Josephus

My book will redeem me.

Mark

But your book seems to make the Romans out to be good and you blame a lot of what happened in the Jewish War on extremist Jews. It seems obvious that you did this to gain favor with the Romans. For example, your description of what happened at Masada is not true. I know that you were not an eyewitness to what happened there; and, also, I heard from a legionnaire, who was actually there, the true story of what really happened.

Josephus

Well the emperor Vespasian had sort of adopted me and I had to write in such a way that didn't antagonize him or his son, Titus. I couldn't very well write how, after dispatching their wives and children, the remaining couple of hundred or so Jews were able to kill over a thousand legionnaires.

Mark

I guess you couldn't. To bring up something else you might have done wrong; I've heard that you have divorced your Jewish wife and married a young, beautiful well-connected Roman woman?

Josephus

Yes, my marriage wasn't going well and my association with Vespasian gave me access to Roman high society with its many beautiful young women. How could I resist?

Mark

I would have.

Josephus

Yes, I've heard that you Christians don't approve of divorce.

Mark

Yes we are against divorce.

Josephus

Each to his own.

Mark

But to get back to your book, why is there no mention of Jesus Christ in your book?

Josephus

I believe that he was the same man as Judas the Galilean, who is in my book.

Mark

That's ridiculous! I never heard of Judas the Galilean until I read your book and certainly don't believe that he and Jesus were the same person.

Josephus

Alright, then why in your book, or the Gospel of Mark as it is now called, is the man called Jesus made out to be more of a religious dissident rather than a political revolutionary like some people think he was?

Mark

Just as you, Josephus, have written your book to make yourself acceptable to Rome, so I, in my account, have done a similar thing to make Jesus, and Christianity in general, acceptable to Rome, by making Jesus out to be only a religious dissident and suppress any indication of his being a political revolutionary.

Josephus

Okay, I understand that. So are you saying that Christianity must be separate from Judaism to avoid Roman antagonism toward the Jews being directed at Christianity?

Mark

Yes, and furthermore, I believe as Paul does that Christianity is for all people and that the large amount of rules and regulations of the religious Jews are too onerous for new converts; and, also, in my opinion, are not necessary in order for people to do justly, be merciful, and do unto others what they would have others do unto them, which are the important essentials of Judaism that I feel Christianity should adopt.

Josephus

But your account puts the blame for the death of Jesus on the Jews. This is not true. Jesus was crucified by the Romans.

The Romans only crucified people who were revolutionaries. Although there were Jews like most Sadducees who disliked Jesus and were in league with the Romans against him.

Mark

Why were the Sadducees so against Jesus?

Josephus

Because Jesus objected strenuously to the profiteering moneylenders in the Temple Court, who were Sadducees, which gave them great power over the ordinary Jews and brought them much wealth through payments for obligatory sacrifices.

Mark

I see.

Josephus

But, I should ask you why is there little or no mention of the enmity of the Sadducees against Jesus in your account? You only write about the Pharisees as the enemy of Jesus, some of whom felt very favorably about Jesus.

Mark

With the destruction of the Temple, the Sadducees disappeared and were no longer worth writing about.

Josephus

I understand. There is another thing that bothers me; namely, that all accounts about Jesus that are written after yours, which is the first to be written, will incorporate your view that the Jews were responsible for the death of Jesus, rather than the Romans; and, as Christianity spreads throughout the Roman Empire, as it seems it will, the antipathy of Christians toward Jews will increase.

Mark

That's possible, but that might be the price that must be paid for Christianity to survive.

Josephus

But what if this leads to outright hatred of Jews by Christians, even to the point of violence? How will you feel about that?

Mark

I repeat, just like you wrote your book to avoid your being censured by Rome, so have I written about Jesus to make Christianity acceptable to Rome.

Josephus

So you are saying that we have both changed history for expediency. But, your account might do the Jewish people a lot more harm than mine will ever do. They might be forever blamed for the death of Jesus because of what you wrote.

Mark

I hope that you are wrong about that.

Josephus

But if I am right, it will be very bad for future Jews.

Mark

Yes, it could be. Let us hope that what I wrote doesn't bode badly for future Jews.

Josephus

I hope so too.

Mark

Time will tell.

Josephus

Yes it will.

(Curtain.)

Printed in the United States
By Bookmasters